MONEY POWER THROUGH MUTUAL FUNDS

Tama McAleese

CHELSEA HOUSE PUBLISHERS
Philadelphia

First published in hardback edition in 1997 by Chelsea House Publishers.

Note: While much careful thought and depth of research have been devoted to the writing of this book, all content is to be viewed as general information only and should not be construed as actual legal, accounting or financial advice of a personal nature. The ideas, suggestions, and general concepts are subject to federal, state, and local laws and statutes. The ever-changing economic, political, and international environment may well demand reinterpretation of some or all of the concepts presented herein.

The reader is urged to consult legal, accounting, and tax advisors regarding all legal and personal financial decisions. This book is not meant to be utilized as a substitute for their advice.

1 3 5 7 9 8 6 4 2

Library of Congress Cataloging-in-Publication Data

      McAleese, Tama.
          Money power through mutual funds / Tama McAleese.
          p.   cm.—(Money Power)
          Includes index.
      ISBN 0-7910-4469-6 (hardcover)
      1. Mutual Funds—United States. 2. Finance, Personal—United States. I. Title II. Series: McAleese, Tama. Money power.
      HG4930.M395   1997
      332.63'27—dc20   96-34782

                              CIP

Table of Contents

MONEY POWER
Through Mutual Funds

Foreword

Once upon a time, a Russian Czar commanded his advisors to seek out and bring back the sum of all knowledge so he could rule as the wisest potentate in history. They spread out across the globe, investigating every civilized society they could reach.

One year later, they returned to their country, carrying voluminous books of information and data. The Czar threw up his hands in frustration—it would take ten lifetimes just to sort through the reams of documents they offered. He demanded they compress this into something smaller and more digestible.

In time, they presented a shorter version to their Czar. Still, it seemed too long to be of immediate use. So the Czar instructed them one last time: be abrupt, if necessary, but get to the point, the bottom line. After all, he had a kingdom to rule over, and he wanted this knowledge put to good use for the benefit of his people.

One advisor finally appeared in the throne room. In his hand was one lonely piece of paper. The Czar, visibly relieved, was even happier when he saw only one sentence on the page. Satisfied that he had found the secret to ultimate wisdom, he rose and read it aloud:

THERE ARE NO FREE LUNCHES.

— Jimmy Warren,Vice President Sales & Marketing, Diamond Products

You can't pick up a magazine or newspaper, turn on the TV or tune in a radio without reading, watching or hearing about mutual funds. I nearly fell out of bed the other night when a recent movie showed a class of high school students rattling off a wish list...and one of the students wished for a mutual fund!

No other investment has created so much excitement and garnered so much interest from the average consumer. At the same time, no other investment has been more misunderstood, misused and abused by the novice investor or been the subject of more myths, fallacies and outright lies.

No wonder the few consumers still hiding in embalmed bank accounts are waiting on the shore, afraid to leave their submerged accounts and swim toward this mysterious life form.

What are these wildly popular investments, how do they work, and are they right for you? **MONEY POWER Through Mutual Funds** tells the real story, in plain English, about every kind of mutual fund. What's more, it presents this information in an easy-to-read and even easier-to-understand question-and-answer format.

A fund for every dream

Do you long for a higher return on your money, wish you could cut out financial middlemen, or dream about diversifying your portfolio like a millionaire? Are you ready to take control of your own money? Are you looking for limited risk to principal, but greater profits on your investments? How about the chance to monitor the performance of your money daily?

Then welcome to the world of mutual funds!

Mutual funds have made it possible for ordinary people to invest in the same instruments as the rich and famous, simply by lowering the ante for getting into the game.

Before the creation of mutual funds, only the rich could play the investing game because the ante was so stiff. A single U.S. Treasury Bill (T-bill) cost nearly $10,000, and the middle class had to find a friend they could trust to purchase even one.

Today, you, the small investor, can easily own a portion of 100 or more T-bills and other U.S. Government agency issues for as little as $25 per month, or with an initial investment of $1,000 or less.

Hire the experts

Through a system called mutual fund investing, small investors can afford to have top professional money managers keep an eye on their portfolios. What's more, companies that offer mutual funds are introducing new services and benefits almost daily.

Mutual fund companies manage your investment money and act as a temporary holding center until you request your account dollars (shares) back. They can keep only expenses and fees that they tell you about beforehand. All other profits (or losses) pass directly to you, the shareholder. So if your mutual fund has a good year, so do you.

The salt of the earth

This book was written for those of you without millions of dollars, nice hard-working folks with no rich Uncle Harry and no trust fund, consumers who face the tremendous challenges of funding college educations for your children or are racing toward retirement age faster than your money is.

This book is especially designed for those of you who are not experts in money management, but, at the same time, are not crazy about the idea of giving your hard-earned dollars to strangers to make investments for you.

Whether you want to invest $250,000, your upcoming lump-sum pension rollover, or the extra $25 per month you've squeezed out of your budget, this book will teach you how to invest like the pros, perhaps even better.

Investing through the mutual-fund system is easy once you know how to play the Mutual Fund Game. And *learning* about money is every bit as important as *earning* it.

Chapter 1

Basic Questions, Basic Answers

The very fact that you've purchased this book means that you have a lot of questions about mutual funds and your over-all investment strategy. So, before we set out on an in-depth discussion of mutual funds—one of *my* favorite topics—I'd like to answer the questions I hear most often from novice investors.

Q: Where do I start?

If you have money that you are ready to invest *now*, there are three things you must do first:

1) Determine what the money will be used *for*. This has a bearing on *when* the money will be needed.

2) Determine the optimum investment vehicle considering the amount of time you'll be able to keep the money invested.

3) Determine the tax benefits of the various options, particularly those you are considering for retirement funds.

For short-term money (needed within three years), the top priority is to **protect the investment principal.** This limits your investment options to bank deposits, certificates of deposit (CDs), or conservative money market mutual funds.

Money that you can tie up for a longer term demands a completely different strategy. Your goal for long-term assets must be to **protect your purchasing power.**

The optimum investment for such long-term money is one that diversifies your investment capital, is not subject to a lot of management expenses, and puts you in control of your funds at all times.

The major advantage of mutual funds is that they diversify your holdings by pooling many investors' assets to purchase more securities. This reduces investment risk. Money market mutual funds are available for short-term money, while a combination of conservative mutual funds will keep your marathon money working as hard as you do.

Mutual funds also are ideal for a variety of tax-advantaged plans such as retirement IRAs, SEPs, KEOGHs, and 401ks. They can be used as custodial accounts for minors and for nonprofit institution tax-deferred annuity programs.

However, you should never let the tax tail wag the investment dog. An investment whose main attraction lies in the tax-free income it generates should be passed up for one of better quality—*even if you have to give up the tax break.*

> **Q:** **Every expert has a different formula or theory for investing. How can a novice find the truth?**

Good money management has not changed much in 50 years. The fundamental principals are quite straightforward:

1. All investments go up and down, including those inside insurance companies, credit unions and banking institutions.

2. Most small investors do the wrong thing at the wrong time.

3. Diversification is the major key to reducing risk.

4. Savings accounts and bank CDs alone will *not* make you rich. They cannot outpace the ravages on your savings brought about by inflation.

5. Uncertainty creates risk, *not* opportunity.

6. No one knows the future, not even so-called money gurus who'll do anything to convince you otherwise.

7. Markets tend to overreact. Never invest out of greed or fear.

8. The bulls make money, and the bears can even glean profits. But the piggies often get slaughtered!!! Leave animals *out* of your investment plans and *in* the barn—you'll have a lot less manure to wade through.

Q: What is a mutual fund?

A mutual fund is not a specific investment like a bank CD or a share of IBM stock. Instead, it is a method of investing money.

Through a mutual fund, you can pool your funds with large and other small investors, hire a top money manager to purchase securities for you, and enjoy the benefits of volume purchasing, selling at a handsome profit and keeping a larger share for yourself. An investment advisor (either an individual or a team) will assume the duties of active management as well as the daily responsibilities for investment decisions.

Today there are nearly 3,700 mutual funds from which to choose. Some of them invest all funds into the stock market. Some avoid stocks altogether, choosing other types of securities, such as U.S. Government or corporate bonds. Many mix and match a combination of stocks, bonds and cash. A few even invest in such diverse and unique investments as gold, real estate, mortgages, or municipality debt of states, cities, and public revenue projects. All of them operate by the same basic rules and regulations.

> **Q: What types of mutual funds are available?**

There are as many categories of mutual funds as there are types of investors. They can be grouped according to their investment strategies and goals and the instruments they purchase:

High-risk stock mutual funds

Maximum capital gains: Funds with this goal invest in high-risk companies and aim for higher returns than the stock market in general.

Small company growth: Funds composed primarily of stocks of companies worth less than $500 million.

Growth: Funds composed primarily of stocks of medium-sized companies expected to grow faster than average.

International: Funds that specialize in stocks of companies outside the U.S.

Precious metals: Funds specializing in stocks of gold, silver or platinum mining companies; few actually hold bullion.

Sector funds: Buy securities from only one industry or market niche.

Medium-risk stock mutual funds

Balanced—typically 60% stocks and 40% bonds.

Growth and income—high-dividend, mature stock companies, bonds and some cash.

Global equity—stocks of both foreign and domestic companies.

Asset allocation—stocks, bonds, cash and gold held in certain percentages that vary with market conditions.

Option income—blue-chip stocks with options to boost the income yield.

Low-risk diversified funds

Equity income—well diversified into many types of securities with a lower percentage in stocks.

High-risk bond funds

High yield (junk) corporates—lower-quality corporate bond obligations.

High yield (junk) municipals—lower-rated municipal bonds issued by cities, states, counties, and revenue or public projects.

International—a portfolio of foreign debt obligations.

Medium-risk bond funds

High grade corporates—higher-quality private company debt.

High grade tax-exempt—better-quality municipal debt bonds.

U.S. Government bonds—protected from default but move up and down in value due to rising or falling interest rates.

Lower-risk bond funds

Short-term taxable—Five to 15-year corporate debt obligations.

Short-term tax-exempt—medium-maturity bonds issued by cities, states, counties and revenue or public projects.

Specialty funds

Mortgage-backed securities—mortgage obligations packaged by brokerages as securities.

Money market funds

Treasury—the safest kind of money market fund because it invests only in U.S. Treasury issues (T-bills).

U.S. Government Agency—not all T-bills; some securities are backed by U.S. agencies, not the government itself.

Taxable—commercial paper IOUs backed by the creditworthiness of the company issuing the short-term debt.

Tax-exempt—short-term municipal debt paper backed by the nonprofit entity or its tax receipts.

Q: Where can I purchase a mutual fund?

Mutual funds are sold directly to you by investment companies or through financial intermediaries such as banks, insurance companies, financial service corporations and brokerages. Before you purchase anything, however, track performance of the funds you've thought, read or heard about to see if they perform better or worse than the market and one another.

Q: Can I purchase a mutual fund over the phone?

Dialing for dollars is a lucrative endeavor of "cold call cowboys." Good mutual funds are *bought* (because of their high-quality, long-term performances), *not* sold (by tele-marketing sales efforts).

Never purchase *any* type of investment via a telephone or newspaper advertisement or solicitation. There are scam artists who make their living from a desk with only a telephone, notepad, marketing list they recently purchased, and a wastebasket full of names of callers who hang up on them.

> **Q: What is the difference between a "front-end load," a "back-end load," and a "no-load" fund?**

There are three ways you wind up paying for a mutual fund. First, there may be an up-front load (sales commission). As we'll discuss more in chapter 4, when you look in the mutual fund tables, you'll find two prices for **front-end load** funds—the buy price and the sell price. The former is always higher than the latter. The difference between these prices—up to 8.5%—is the sales commission you're paying *up-front*.

Rather than an up-front commission, some funds charge a **back-end load**—i.e., you pay the commission when you *sell* your shares. In many cases, those sales commissions are reduced, year by year, the longer you hold the fund. Eventually, there may be no obvious commission at all.

(Some funds may be bought either way. If this is the case, the up-front load fund will be called "A," and the back-end load fund, "B.")

No-load funds charge no commission when you buy, no commission when you sell. They are marked in the newspaper "NL."

As we'll see later, however, even no-load funds are charging you *some*thing for the privilege of investing. After all, there *is* no free lunch, is there?

> **Q: What services and customer benefits**
> **can I expect from mutual funds?**

The following is just a partial list of benefits and services today's mutual fund investor can find:

1) 24-hour access to account information and other data;

2) Check-writing privileges for 24-hour banking;

3) Daily account monitoring in the newspaper;

4) Wire transfers directly to and from your local lending institution;

5) Transfers between funds in the same mutual fund family;

6) Automatic monthly income sent to your home or bank;

7) Account link-ups with your banking institution;

8) Regular account statements and fund updates:

9) Prompt distribution of dividends, interest and capital gains;

10) Free reinvesting of dividends, interest and capital gains;

11) Retirement plans such as IRA accounts, SEPs, KEOGHs, and 403b tax-deferred annuities for nonprofit organizations;

12) Tax-advantaged college savings programs such as Uniform Gift to Minors (UGMA);

13) Automatic monthly investment programs;

14) Payroll deduction plans;

15) 24-hour communication with your mutual fund;

16) Quick redemption of your account via telephone instructions;

17) Telephone transfers to other funds;

18) Simple, easy-to-read reports, records and tax statements;

19) All investor privileges regardless of how little you invest;

20) Certificates of ownership (if desired);

21) Easy investing procedures;

22) Fast telephone liquidations of account funds;

23) Direct liquidations back to the fund;

24) Joint-ownership accounts;

25) Reader-friendly periodic reports.

Q: Is mutual fund investing fail-safe?

We become successful investors because:

1) We research and investigate thoroughly before we ever invest our precious investment funds;

2) We never invest out of greed or fear;

3) We avoid management fees and expenses, eliminate financial middlemen, and go directly to the investments themselves;

4) We always purchase on the basis of quality, not price;

5) We diversify our investment eggs into many baskets;

6) We understand the structure of a mutual fund—what it can promise and what are its limitations;

7) We are prudent investors with realistic expectations regarding future performance;

8) We invest conservatively;

9) We choose a fund whose investment policies are consistent with our risk tolerance and personal financial goals;

10) We are loyal investors—we stay with a fund for the long-term;

11) We become systematic savers;

12) We ignore those products sold on the basis of high yields or last year's performance numbers.

Now that I've answered some of your preliminary questions, let's take a detailed look in the next chapter about investment strategies for your short-term money.

Chapter 2

Investing Your Short-term Funds

As we discussed in Chapter 1, you must devise two very different money strategies for short-term vs. your long-term investing.

Every household should aim to have money for the rainy day on which the pink slip arrives and the transmission falls out of the car. That's when you'll need access to liquid funds in short-term investments.

In plotting your strategy, think of short-term funds as those you might need within a three-year time period. Besides the rainy-day money, these funds could cover Christmas or next summer's vacation, a new car, starting your own business, or saving a down payment for a new home.

Short-term money can also include larger financial goals that are less than three years away. College might be lurking around the corner, or retirement might be on the horizon. The nature of the financial goals is secondary to the time frame the money has to work before it is needed.

Once we isolate short-term money from long-term assets, we are better able to choose the best mutual funds to achieve those goals.

Liquidity and marketability

Short-term savings should be limited to investments offering liquidity and marketability. Marketability means that the investment can sell quickly, while liquidity implies that every dollar invested can be retrieved without worrying about loss of principal.

Of course, the conservative nature of this tactic rules out many hotly advertised investments touting higher current yields since they put your principal at greater risk of loss.

Therefore, for short-term funds I recommend a combination of money market mutual funds, bank CDs, savings accounts, bank money market accounts, and savings bonds already purchased for short-term financial goals.

The investment vehicles I recommend are the dull, four-door sedans of the investment world. Because the return *of* your money is more important over the short time period than the return *on* your money.

Q: What exactly is a money market mutual fund?

A money market mutual fund is a large pool of investor money managed by an investment company. It seeks short-term interest on assets as well as conservation of investment principal.

Although there is no guarantee that any money market will accomplish its investment objectives, money market funds invest only in short-term securities, thus reducing one of the greatest risk factors in the world of investing—time.

Recent securities laws have required money market mutual funds to upgrade their selection of securities and shorten the length of time until maturity. They are now confined to purchasing only higher-quality debt obligations.

Larger corporations, the U.S. Government, and even state and local municipalities borrow large sums for short periods by issuing IOUs in return for cash. These debts are considered low risk because of their short duration. Loans may mature overnight, last for a week, or mature as far into the future as a year. But money market mutual fund assets are traditionally positioned in shorter issues, averaging 30-60 days to maturity.

The U.S. Government borrows by issuing **Treasury bills** (T-bills) and **federal agency notes**.

Private companies issue IOUs called **commercial paper**.

Banks borrow by offering larger **certificates of deposit** (CDs).

And city, state and public projects sell paper called **TANs, RANs** and **BANs.**

Since these instruments are short-term, their yields are relatively low.

The average consumer is shut out of this investment opportunity because T-bills are priced at almost $10,000 a pop, while jumbo bank CDs are packaged at $100,000 each. You would have to organize the entire neighborhood to purchase any of the larger pools of debt securities yourself!

But by gathering investor funds together, mutual fund companies enable small investors to purchase T-bills, CDs and other securities in proportion to the number of shares they contribute to the total investment pot.

Money market funds are designed for the maximum returns achievable given the specific risk. On the surface, they may all look alike. So your tendency may be to choose from the highest yields, as you do when you shop for your own CDs and savings accounts. However, be careful. Unlike those instruments, money market mutual funds are *not* guaranteed by the FDIC or any agency of the government. Therefore, you must evaluate the riskiness of funds advertising those higher returns.

What's in a name?

Money market mutual funds originally generated so much appeal that banks started offering a special account bearing the same name. However, a *bank* money market savings account has little in common with a *real* money market mutual fund.

Money market mutual funds follow the general rules and policies as other mutual funds in terms of legal structure, operating practices and consumer disclosure. Each money market fund offers an investment prospectus, outlining all pertinent data and information—very helpful once you can decipher what foreign language they are speaking.

Read this prospectus carefully and thoroughly understand every word before sending any money to a money market or, for that matter, any other mutual fund company. (How to use a mutual fund prospectus is more thoroughly explained in Chapter 5.)

Q: What types of money market funds can I choose from?

There are taxable money markets that invest only in U.S. Government Treasuries, or its agencies or both. There are others that maintain higher yields by avoiding lower-yielding U.S. securities and investing only in private corporate commercial paper (IOUs).

The very highest yields are achieved through foreign (global) debt securities and short-term foreign bonds issued by their respective governments or companies. Since these have greater risk to principal, their yields are more attractive. They are also vulnerable to wide swings on the currency exchange markets as one country's currency moves up and another declines in value.

Municipalities such as states, cities, counties and public projects issue debt paper in the form of tax-exempt securities. Called tax-exempt money markets, they are subject to credit changes and the general financial health of their issuer. The yields are lower, but the earnings are not taxable by the federal government.

Sometimes you can get double tax savings if you purchase securities issued by your home state (which are then exempt from state taxes too).

> **Q: What kind of sales charges, manage-
> ment expenses and fees should I ex-
> pect to pay?**

Since it's relatively simple to buy and sell U.S. government issues and short-term commercial paper, the administration costs and management fees of money market funds should be low.

Look for money market funds that charge no up-front fees to start, no ongoing distribution (12b-1) charges, and less than 3/4 of 1% total expenses. Brokerages often sell money market accounts with a small but tacky underlying commission. Avoid these.

The fund you choose should also offer free transactions, unlimited check-writing, and all the regular services of the mutual fund family. Use funds with low required minimum check amounts.

> **Q: What are the advantages and bene-
> fits of investing in these funds?**

You get professional management. But don't get carried away—it doesn't take a rocket scientist or money guru to buy and sell short-term securities (unless clever strategies and trading are being employed that will only increase the volatility of your principal).

And you can purchase better yields because of the economies of scale derived by pooling investor funds.

Finally, management fees should be low because as the fund size increases, many expenses are reduced.

Q: Do I need a lot of money up-front?

There are usually low minimum requirements to open a money market fund, such as $1,000. Some offer an automatic monthly investment plan so you can start with as little as $25 per month. If your account later dips below the required minimum, you can usually maintain your account and continue the benefits of daily compounded interest and check-writing privileges.

Q: Are there disadvantages or limitations to investing in these funds?

No investment is perfect, and money markets are no exception. Since the funds are invested in only shorter-term issues, the yields are relatively low and will not outpace inflation over long periods of time. They must be coupled with other types of mutual funds to provide some growth of capital.

Money market mutual funds are not insured as a whole by the government or any of their agencies, even though they may contain government issues such as Treasury bills or Ginnie Maes. Therefore, a good consumer must look to the underlying issues to determine their quality and, subsequently, the safety of their principal.

I recommend that you seek only those money market funds that invest wholly in U.S. T-Bills and U.S. agency paper.

Q: Can these funds' check-writing privileges replace my checking account?

Money market funds usually maintain low expenses and attempt to reduce costs by restricting how little you can withdraw (redeem) at a time. Most require that you write a check for at least $100 or more. Some have even increased that figure to $500 per check.

It would be foolish to write a money market check for more than you currently need when you could be making daily interest instead. It is usually not feasible to write checks out for more than your actual purchase. So do not rely on a money market fund for ordinary expenses such as groceries, gasoline, etc.

Q: My tax bite is killing me. Can a money market provide any relief?

Tax-free money market funds are popular—for obvious reasons. They are not taxed by the federal government. If they are bought in the same state in which they are issued, they may also be free of state taxes. This "free lunch" is compromised by the accompanying lower yield (because the earnings are tax-exempt). Since issuers can offer the tax advantage, they don't have to pay investors as much to entice them.

Investors in high tax brackets often compare the yields on tax-free funds with returns of taxable money markets and choose on that basis only. However, there is a compelling argument against tax-free (municipal bond) money markets.

The underlying securities are not backed by the federal government or any of its agencies but, rather, by cities, counties, states, hospitals, schools, revenue projects, and public institutions saddled by problems caused by cutbacks in federal and state funding.

The credit ratings on some bonds have already declined, making them less desirable and decreasing their value. As we grope toward a national system of health care and struggle to repair our ailing economy, municipal bonds are not a dependable safety net for anyone's emergency or sock fund.

While it is true that *no* money market, taxable or tax-free, has yet defaulted on its shareholders to date, past performance is no guarantee of future results.

Q: How safe are these funds?

Not long ago, that question would not have been asked. In 1990, however, several large companies defaulted on their short-term debt owed to a dozen money market funds. The funds covered the losses, but the scare was enough to prompt investors to look for more than a high yield in selecting a fund.

Pick a relatively large (but not behemoth) fund. While size doesn't always signify greater safety, a mid-size fund can purchase a greater number of issues to diversify against the default of one or more issuers.

Sufficient size might also help a fund weather mass investor exits (redemptions) better than a fund with a smaller asset base (fewer securities) and less ready cash on hand.

You should also be wary of those funds that compete by lowering expenses while pinching profit margins. This strategy is only temporarily effective and can come back to bite the manager if greedy investors threaten to leave when expenses have to be increased at a later date.

In addition, examine the debt ratings in the prospectus and favor those funds with substantial positions in Treasury bills and U.S. government agency issues—these decrease the risk of default.

Do not reach for a slightly higher yield at greater risk to your principal. Money market mutual funds are designed for safety first, not yield or return.

Q: What else can I do to increase safety?

Analyze maturity averages. The shorter the maturity of the securities, the less vulnerable a fund is to default risk. Consider only those money market funds that do *not* allow trading of any of the securities inside the portfolio. Otherwise it is possible to lose principal if interest rates move in an unexpected direction as well as from default by an issuer.

You should also check the statement of investments to see what foreign debt a money market might have purchased. Are you comfortable if some of your liquid assets are invested in a Japanese bank, an Australian waterworks revenue project, or a Philippine railroad? Probably not.

Therefore, you should stick to those money markets that invest heavily in our own debt-ridden government, its agencies or instrumentalities. Global securities can suffer from currency exchange and the market adjustments (or crises) that often occur in these less stable countries. Don't let anyone convince you that investing in foreign bonds is simply smarter banking.

Q: Can I open a money market fund with my spouse or child, as I can a regular checking account?

Yes, but be mindful of the liability obligations and potential limitations regarding joint ownership of securities.

Checks can be instantly written against the value of your fund as they can with a regular checking account. If you open the money market in multiple names, you will have a joint ownership relationship with all other owners on the account.

This is called *joint tenancy with rights of survivorship* and is a bit different than a traditional bank survivorship account.

If your application declares that only one signature is required for account redemptions (withdrawals), an individual account owner can write checks without the permission or knowledge of any other account holder. (That means your kid or spouse could go on a spending spree without your ever knowing...until the monthly statement came.)

Each joint owner has full privileges regarding deposits, withdrawals and shareholder rights. In other words, each joint owner owns 100% of the assets in the account.

To protect your account against unauthorized withdrawals without your written consent, you can require that each owner's signature appear on every withdrawal request, whether by check, letter or telephone.

For the student away from home

While your student is away at college, a jointly owned money market fund between parent and child, with one signature required for withdrawal, can give instant cash for tuition, books and living expenses. The parent sends appropriate deposits to the fund. The child redeems what is needed by writing checks on the share balance. (Sounds just like home again, doesn't it?)

A parent can monitor the checking activity and spending habits of his or her student through the monthly statements from the fund, which show all deposits, any interest credited, all checks written, and any other type of redemption procedure or fee. Until the student actually spends the money, it continues to gain daily current interest.

The parents can maintain some control over the assets by limiting the amount they deposit. Some mutual funds even offer overnight options so you can wire money from your local bank or checking account if the occasional crisis call comes in at the eleventh hour from the campus end.

> **Q: So a money market mutual fund is the right place for my emergency money?**

Everyone must have rainy-day money. With increased concern over both the domestic and international economies, it is prudent to maintain such a "sock fund" now. Some bank CDs or savings, a solid money market mutual fund with check-writing privileges *outside* a banking institution, and a few savings bonds may help you sleep better until our economy is running more like the well-oiled machine of the American spirit.

Chapter 3

Strategies For Long-term Money

College educations for the kids. Retirement and the "golden years."

These are the most common goals people have for their long-term investments. Since time can be either a great friend or relentless enemy to your long-term money, you must choose your investments wisely. The right mutual funds are the best place to park your money. Which ones are safe? What are the strategies you should use in selecting your fail-safe portfolio?

In this chapter we will answer some of the most common questions about the right investments for so-called "marathon money."

> **Q: Are mutual funds better for a college fund than savings bonds and bank deposits?**

If high school graduation is at least three years away, mutual funds can offer an excellent inflation hedge against escalating college costs.

You cannot successfully chase a college tuition bill increasing by 8% to 12% per year with savings bonds or bank certificates of deposit, even if the bonds can be bought tax-free. You need a stronger inflation fighter.

The best gift you could give your pink or blue bundle at birth is $25 or $50 per month in a growth mutual fund (one with lots of stocks inside). When the account becomes larger and has a good year, transfer your stake into a more conservative type of fund.

Develop a consistent monthly investing program using *dollar-cost-averaging*—investing a fixed amount of money on a regular basis so you purchase more shares when the price is low, fewer as prices rise. This allows the magic of compounding to work its miracles.

You can supercharge your college investment by attaching a Uniform Gift to Minor tax shelter until your child reaches his or her age of majority. This allows you to make a gift of the investment dollars to your children and shift the tax consequences to their lower tax bracket. An adult custodian (who could be you) chooses both the investment and how the money is spent for the child.

Since this is a legal gift for tax purposes, you can't take it back later. No Indian-giving. In addition, you are not allowed to convince your child to fund Christmas vacation in the Alps for the family. The purpose of the money must remain for the benefit of the child, with the exception of elementary support costs. (See my second book, ***Money: How To Get It, Keep It, And Make It Grow,*** for more information on custodial accounts.)

When your student enters college, switch some of his or her funds to a money market mutual fund with check-writing privileges. This allows either you or your student 24-hour access to needed money while you continue to earn valuable interest on the account.

Q: Can I use mutual funds for my IRA account?

An IRA (Individual Retirement Account) is merely a tax benefit wrapped around the investment of your choice. For example, a bank IRA is usually a certificate of deposit with the letters "I-R-A" stamped on it. An insurance company IRA is really an insurance annuity contract labeled "IRA." The terms IRA, SEP, KEOGH, TSA, 403b or 401k do not refer to the investments themselves.

Mutual funds are ideal for IRA accounts. They diversify even a limited amount of money into many smaller types of investment to reduce risk. They eliminate extra management expense and costs that alternative institutions such as banks and insurance companies charge you.

Since IRA contributions are longer-term investments, your principal can fluctuate as long as your long-term goal—growth to act as a hedge against inflation—is met.

> **Q: Aren't mutual funds risky? I don't feel secure putting my savings into the stock market.**

The stock market *can* be treacherous, but there is no such thing as a no-risk investment.

The trick is to balance the importance of conserving your principal while building future purchasing power. Manage risk through prudent investing in conservative funds that invest only a portion of their total assets in individual stocks.

Also bear in mind that investing only for safety of principal is the primary reason so many of today's elderly are virtually living in poverty. They allowed inflation to eat away at their savings as their money sat in safe, low- or no-growth investment instruments.

The greatest financial blunder a retiree can make is to ignore inflation, drawing their money around them like some protective cloak, as if they had barely six months to live.

The main focus of retirement investing must be the pre-servation of purchasing power. You cannot stave off inflation by investing only in fixed-income vehicles such as bank de-posits, bonds and fixed-income insurance products.

Research and monitor conservative mutual funds—such as equity income types—that hang together during stagnant or declining market conditions, yet outpace inflation during the booms.

Such funds will have some CDs, some cash, perhaps Treasury bills, a few familiar stocks, corporate bonds, even some U.S. government bonds. They are a kind of financial stew and diversify to protect against risk as well as any millionaire's portfolio could. Take your time and slowly move a portion of your assets into these all-weather veterans. You will be much better prepared at retirement time.

Remember: inflation will never go away. So always man-age some of your money for future growth, no matter what your age.

Q: I'm too old to worry about inflation; I need safety. Are you suggesting I risk my principal?

Inflation, the deadliest money-killer over long periods of time, will not pass over your home. It is in your refrigerator in the form of higher food prices, in your gas tank and moving through your heating and air conditioning ducts, hiding there in higher energy costs. It is lurking invisibly in the escalating cost for health care.

Unless you are down to your last few thousand dollars, structure your investments using the "financial bicycle" concept, positioning your assets into three basic categories: bank deposits backed by the FDIC, a money market mutual fund investing only in U.S. government short-term (less than one year) securities, and equity income mutual funds.

Avoid large investments in bond funds, adjustable-rate mortgage funds, Ginnie Maes, international bonds, and long-term government bond funds. They automatically lose principal when current interest rates move up. By putting all your funds into only one type of investment vehicle, you will lose the diversification you need to weather all types of market adjustments.

> **Q: Considering the uncertain economy, is it prudent to invest now for the long-term at all?**

Do you believe your government can continue to bail out banks, savings and loans, and insurance companies, pay off mounting deficit debt, provide increased social programs like national health care, support increasingly sagging and underfunded pension funds, fill favored sacred-cow coffers to buy popularity and campaign chests for election votes, *and have anything left over for your old age?!?*

Right! At least put in that annual IRA contribution, tax-deductible or not!

> **Q: I'm retiring soon. How can I make bigger profits and get rich quicker?**

You don't need a financial planner, you need Rumple-stiltskin, who can spin straw into gold. If you are already concerned that you won't have enough money for the future, how can you afford to lose what you have now in an effort to make money faster?

To catch a mouse, the saying goes, one must first behave like cheese. Get-rich-quick themes and schemes from money gurus who offer fast profits are a direct route to getting poor, whether overnight or over time. Exposing your precious capital to greater risk usually nets larger losses, not faster gains. Go for the gold in some other area of your life and stay satisfied with steady progress from slow and solid investment vehicles. Manage your wealth like you would your own business—very, very carefully.

Q: My IRA accounts are with banks and insurance companies. Can I move them into mutual funds?

Your insurance annuity can be transferred by requesting an account surrender in writing. If you are told you will in- cur severe surrender charges by moving now, realize that any such charges are really the fees charged when you originally invested. That money is already gone—into the pockets of both the agent and the company. You opted for the free lunch, believing that someone would invest your money for nothing, and these internal charges are coming back to haunt you.

Do not be frightened (by the fear of loss) into staying with a ·mediocre investment until deferred expenses wear off. That could take years and will only put you further behind in your race against inflation via a better return.

You might also have to pay a 10% penalty to the IRS for withdrawing your annuity funds before age 59 1/2. Remember the agent who sold you this plan and how well he or she was paid to seduce you into an inflexible vehicle with no back-door escape hatch. Next time ask probing questions regarding the cost of saying "goodbye" to an investment company. When you dance for free, you eventually pay the piper.

You have only 60 days from the date you receive your IRA check to roll over your savings into another investment. If you miss your 60-day transfer deadline you will lose the IRA tax benefit and all money will become taxable in that year.

You should wait until your CD matures to roll over your savings into a mutual fund. Otherwise you may incur early-withdrawal penalties. Many lending institutions currently offer penalty-free withdrawals for senior citizens. Check your bank for a list of withdrawal privileges and penalties.

Copy everything for your files, including the IRA mutual fund application and the front and back of your check. This establishes a clear paper trail in case the IRS should question your transfer at a later time. Always send important documents via certified mail, return receipt requested.

Keep the IRA rollover accounts separate from other mutual fund money, even if you invest all your savings in the same mutual fund. You want to maintain separate numbers for each account. Opening an additional account is prudent to maintain a clear photo of your retirement moves over time. The better the paper trail, the easier you can defend your actions in ten or fifteen years if there should be any question. Better safe than sorry.

> **Q: How often can I change my IRA account to another investment vehicle?**

If you had nothing better to do, you could transfer from place to place on a daily basis. However, tax law only allows one check sent directly to you each 365 days. To transfer more often, simply request a direct transfer of funds to the new investment company or mutual fund.

To transfer an IRA situated for more than one year in a specific vehicle, complete the transaction within 60 days from the date you receive your check. Most investment companies recommend you use a trustee-to-trustee transfer process. But consider intervening by receiving your rollover check and sending it yourself to the new mutual fund company. That way you can direct it from the original custodian through to the new one. Otherwise, you could get caught in the middle, with the old company claiming it sent the money to the new custodian and the new trustee protesting it never received the funds.

If the new company does not notify you within 30 days of the receipt of your funds, call and, if necessary, contact the old institution to stop payment on the check they issued. Ask them to start over and redo the entire transaction.

Reissuing a stopped check is simpler than retracing last month's ledger sheets and redemption orders through a backroom accounting department, especially when the original company (that lost your account) has no motivation to find the error.

To move your funds more often than annually, you must move from one trustee directly to another via a special form. This IRS restriction prevents investors from taking short-term loans on their IRA accounts on a regular basis.

> **Q: What are the tax rules when I invest my IRA in a mutual fund?**

The tax laws are the same no matter what investment vehicle you choose for an IRA account.

Current IRA law limits some taxpayers' ability to deduct the full amount of an annual IRA. See your tax advisor for the latest information.

Remember that since an IRA protects your investment from current taxation, any losses sustained are not tax deductible because any profits are not taxed either. You could lose principal in a mutual fund, even though it is an IRA account. So invest carefully in conservative funds, and structure your investment portfolio for slow and steady gains over time.

> **Q: I can't have an IRA any more because I have a pension plan at work. What can I do?**

Anyone who works and earns a paycheck can have an IRA account. The only tax change refers to whether your annual contribution can be deducted directly off the gross income on your tax return.

Unfortunately, Congress lets no good deal go unpunished for very long. So for some the tax deduction that felt so good and erased a maximum of $2,000 per worker off that W-4 has been maimed by the 1986 Tax Act. But the death of the IRA has been greatly exaggerated.

> **Q: Since I can't deduct my IRA contributions (I have a pension plan *and* I make too much money), why bother?**

Suppose a taxpayer makes an annual $2,000 *totally non-deductible* IRA contribution each year as opposed to merely investing $2,000 per year in a taxable investment. Both the non-deductible IRA and the taxable investment capital are invested in the same investment vehicle averaging 10% per year. But the IRA has the advantage of tax-deferred profits year after year. The following is the result of each investment at the end of 20 and 30 years:

At the end of:	Non-deductible IRA	Taxable Investment
20 years	$126,005	$ 84,272
30 years	$361,887	$189,588

* I have assumed our mythical taxpayer is in the 28% marginal tax bracket and pays an additional 5% in state and local taxes.

The longer the period during which money can compound, the larger the gap between the IRA total and that of the taxable investment.

If any portion of the IRA account can be deducted, the advantages over time will be even *greater!*

Deposit the maximum into that IRA every year, deductible or not.

IRA tax law will continually change as Congress seeks revenues at the expense of long-term planning for retirees. Even if the IRA remains totally non-deductible to some (see your tax advisor for current tax rules), your earnings will remain tax-deferred so you will not have to share any profits with Uncle Sam until retirement time.

The difference between a tax-sheltered investment and a similar taxable investment is so significant over time that to eliminate a non-deductible IRA could cost you $100,000 or more for your retirement pot, depending on your age.

Q: If I retire, become disabled or change employment, should I roll my pension fund into an IRA and invest it in mutual funds?

Your retirement dollars are the most serious money you will ever produce. A stranger has been investing your nest egg for years, most likely without your knowledge of where and how well it was being managed. If the company offers a lump-sum option, consider taking charge of your own assets.

Maybe you were too busy making those original seed dollars to take the time to manage them. But three hot meals a day and a comfortable roof over your head will depend on how well those funds perform from now on. *You have nothing more important to do than to learn how to watch over your own retirement pot.*

Diversify your retirement funds into a combination of bank deposits, a money market mutual fund that invests only in U.S. government issues, and those dull, boring, and stodgy mutual fund turtles, the equity income types, along with a seasoning of a global fund.

With this combination you can manage your money like a pro—perhaps even better.

Q: Should I take my pension as a lump sum or through monthly distribution?

Choosing the monthly pension income payout instead of the one-time lump sum may limit your freedom to change your mind later. What if you need medical care your health insurance won't cover? How will you handle a large unexpected financial crisis? What if you want an extra vacation?

Choosing an irrevocable monthly income option adds another shrinking monthly check for inflation to eat away at. With projected health-care costs at astronomical levels, you will need the flexibility to take your money as you need it, *when* you need it.

Could your company fly south of the border with the Canadian geese one winter? How will you cope if the promises made to retirees and their families become greater than pension assets can produce? As more and more workers consider longer retirements, long-term pension promises are tremendous risks, especially if you don't have a seat on the company's board of directors or an executive's golden parachute.

Occasionally, a company's lump-sum offer is so paltry compared to the monthly income option that you have little choice but to pick monthly payments for the remainder of your life. Lump-sum offers to employees may begin to decrease as liquidations on pension-fund payouts bulge.

Before you make a final election that could be irrevocable, get a tax advisor or real financial planner to calculate the lump-sum potential at a current interest rate invested by you and paid out over your lifetime. Compare these figures with the monthly payment retirement plan. This number-crunching is vital and should not be combined with your purchase of any financial product or investment.

Get only the figures at this time—ignore all sales pitches. It is dangerous to your financial health to dangle a large retirement pot in front of a hungry product vendor. Money can calm the nerves, but it also attracts the vultures.

> **Q:** **Where can I get higher yields *and* safety of principal *and* inflation protection?**

You will be the first person to whom I reveal this top secret investment...as soon as I have made more money than I will ever need.

There is no Santa Claus, no tooth fairy, and no perfect investment that can give it all to you.

Sacrifice some *safety* of principal to achieve more *growth* of principal. Liquidate or withdraw what you need from your total investment account instead of hunting higher yields with dubious promises of safety and higher monthly income checks.

> **Q:** **I am retired and need to supplement my monthly income. Can mutual funds help?**

...ual funds have a variety of monthly withdrawal op-
...ons. You can request any dividends, monthly interest and/or
capital gains sent to you instead of reinvesting them into your
account. If you have more than one type of fund, you might
want to choose a portion from each fund sent to you on a
regular basis.

You can also arrange to have a specific dollar amount
sent to you or deposited directly into your checking account
monthly.

If you need additional money (or less than anticipated),
simply call your fund and request an adjustment. This can
usually be processed by the next month.

If you are withdrawing from an IRA account, your fund
may ask for written notice. At all times, IRA rules supersede
any mutual-fund policies. Shareholder services can give you
details about their particular redemption policies.

If you are younger than age 59 1/2 but need a monthly
income now, you may be eligible for early withdrawals from
your IRA account *without* incurring a 10% penalty. You must
provide your fund with written notice and specify how much
can be redeemed under the law that allows this benefit. This
early withdrawal provision of the tax law allows an IRA
owner under 59 1/2 to take substantially equal payments
without penalty (not without income taxes) based on their
future life expectancy.

Once started, the withdrawals must last until age 59 1/2 or
for five years (whichever is longer). After age 59 1/2 (or five
years), there are no penalties on withdrawals—just income
taxes. Any early withdrawal option plan should be assessed
by your tax expert before implementing. Accurate figures are
critical, as withdrawing too much or too little can have nega-
tive tax consequences.

If you don't need regular income but do need to tap into
your savings occasionally, don't request a withdrawal option.
Money you don't currently use will languish if stored in
today's embalmed savings accounts. Allow your funds to compound as long as possible before requesting them. Most
mutual funds allow telephone redemptions (liquidations) with

checks posted the following day. In the corporate world, this is called "just in time" delivery: you want your money delivered to you "just in time" for your spending purposes.

Perhaps you need more income than your specific mutual fund throws off in interest, dividends and capital gains distributions.

If you are investing for some growth of principal, you can request the earnings without dipping into your investment principal. If that is insufficient, tighten your budget belt a bit and request just a little more in your monthly check, even though you may start cutting into investment principal.

Retirees dread this more than receding gums because this is money that will never again compound for future yields. If they dip into principal long enough, their savings will eventually be wiped out.

Too many elderly search out, instead, financial products that advertise higher yields. Be careful. Higher returns most often signal increased risk to investment principal. A better compromise is to do what I've stressed throughout this chapter, if at all possible: stay with more solid and more diversified investments and conserve spending.

Q: How long must I keep my IRA account records?

For the rest of your life or eternity, whichever is longer. Most mutual funds provide a year-end statement that summarizes the year's activities, including contributions, redemptions and sources of profit. Keep all of them...every year.

If the IRS should ever doubt your reporting, the burden of proof is on *you,* and there are significant penalties and tax consequences if you cannot show where your IRA accounts moved and other important data.

> **Q: I'm only 22. Retirement is 40+ years away. When should I start investing in an IRA account?**

There are three basic restrictions on money: (1) the number of years it can compound before you need it; (2) the rate of return or yield you receive on it; and (3) how much of it you must share with Uncle Sam in the form of annual taxes on your profits.

The more time you have until retirement, the more awesome the concept of compounding becomes. Contribute $2,000 per year to an IRA account yielding 10% annually until age 67 (your full retirement age for Social Security purposes), and your money will grow to $1,581,591. If you can increase your annual return to 12% per year, your total accumulation will be $3,042,435! The longer the time allowed for compounding, the more powerful the results.

Now for the bad news: those figures do not reflect any taxes you may pay on an annual basis. The IRA to the rescue! An IRA account will shelter your profits from yearly taxes until you withdraw your money after retirement.

In the 28% marginal tax bracket, the effects of deferring taxation on your retirement savings are startling: a 10% return taxed at 28% yields only 7.2% per year and total savings at age 67 of only $650,455 (instead of $1,581,591). Increasing your rate of return to 12% per year helps. But you can still build up only $1,022,089 (compared to $3,042,435 without the tax limitations). The underlying investment vehicle remains the same, but the larger savings is marked "IRA," while the taxable account is at the mercy of the taxman.

A small amount of money, worked over a long period of time at a competitive rate without current taxation, can yield the miracles you will need for retirement. Inflation will seriously erode your purchasing power over the years. So there will never be a better time, a cheaper time, or a more profitable time than *now* to invest for your retirement.

Chapter 4

Tracking Your Mutual Funds

What section of the newspaper do you open to first? The sports pages? Horoscope? Bridge column? Crossword?

Well, things are about to change. Once you get involved in the world of mutual funds, you'll share the fun of tracking the investments you are thinking about choosing.

In this chapter, we'll discuss some of the fun of following mutual funds and what you might look for before you select a fund or family of funds.

Let the games begin!

Q: How do I track my mutual fund in the newspaper? The financial pages are so confusing.

Many newspapers publish a daily "Mutual Funds" section or page; nearly all of them give a summary of the week's activity in the Sunday edition.

Turn to the mutual fund page and find the alphabetical listing of the parent group or mutual fund family that offers the specific fund you wish to track. You will see an abbreviated version of the fund's name (e.g., Gwth for Growth Fund, CaTE for California Tax-exempt, G&I for Growth and Income, etc.).

The pluses and minuses of mutual funds

You may see a "High" and a "Low" price or just one price, then a (+) or (-) figure after that. If there are two prices beside the mutual fund, the higher one is the "buy" price—what you would have to pay per share to buy the fund—and the lower one is the "sell" price—what you could get if you wished to sell one or more shares. The difference between these two is the unseen but always applicable "load"—the price you're paying for the privilege of buying that fund.

When a fund shows only one price per share, it has no visible charge when it is purchased.

You can track the performance of the fund in the change column. The figures are calculated in cents. A "—.02" means the fund lost two cents a share during the time period reported.

How should you react to your fund's inevitable ups and downs? Well, you should certainly be happy about large (+) numbers, but you should also feel confident if you see only small (-) figures when overall markets are having a bad day.

Mutual funds do not work on a time clock like a bank CD or other type of guaranteed-return account. Eventually, you'll become comfortable with periodic changes and take a longer term view in evaluating fund performance.

Give us a sign

There may be other symbols beside your fund:

(r) Indicates a redemption fee might apply when you liquidate your shares. This surrender charge might decline over several years or it may remain fixed over the life of your fund investment.

(p) Indicates periodic distribution expenses may be charged after the original sale. They might be as small as 1/4%, as large as 2%. These pay for marketing expenses and are called 12b-1 charges.

(x) Means the fund has just distributed a dividend and is trading without the amount of the dividend it credited to shareholders.

(e) Signifies that the fund has just distributed a capital gain to shareholders and the price is shown without the capital gains.

(t) Means the fund has both a 12b-1 plan and back-load redemption fees.

If two prices appear side by side, the net asset value, or liquidation price, is the lower one. If only one price appears, the buy and sell price are the same. When an "r" is listed after the single price, redemption charges (a back load) are applicable.

Multi-tracking

Spend some time tracking several funds. If one is truly a quality veteran, it will still be healthy and available in three months or six months. *Do not* rush your selection. Give each fund time to strut its stuff or stumble.

You might also compare a riskier fund such as a 100% stock or bond fund in your charts to see how those funds move in comparison to a well-diversified one. You will note larger movements in the former due to the lack of diversification into several types of investments. You can compare risk levels, especially when the minus signs abound. All investments go down. The concern is: how much?

Q: How else can I track my funds?

Many funds provide a 24-hour information system for access to your fund account and market information. You can call the toll-free (800) access number and choose from the following menus:

1) Fund prices and a complete listing of all funds managed by the mutual fund company;

2) The daily change in net asset value (share price) from the day before;

3) The latest dividend, interest and/or capital gain information for your fund;

4) Your account balance and the most current market value;

5) Data on your most recent account transaction;

6) Information regarding the most recent dividend reported;

7) Check-writing information on your account;

8) An overview of current market conditions, sometimes recorded by one of the portfolio managers;

9) Transaction instructions, including how to purchase additional shares, how to redeem or liquidate from your account, and how to transfer part or all of your shares to another mutual fund in the same fund family;

10) Tax excerpts about your 1099-DIV, 1099-B or Form 1099-R.

There are many other convenient services mutual funds offer busy and active investors. You could soak in your tub, relax by the pool, or drive in your car while receiving up-to-the-minute status reports on your investments.

> **Q: What sorts of statements and notices can I expect from the fund company?**

Your mutual fund company will send you an account statement every time some financial activity occurs. When there is a distribution of dividends, interest or capital gains, for example, you will receive notice of how much and whether it was reinvested back to buy additional new shares or sent by check to your current address of record.

A statement will automatically be generated whenever you invest money or request a redemption withdrawal. An end-of-the-year statement will provide an easy-to-read picture of your entire year's account activity.

Not all funds invest in securities that distribute a regular source of income to their investors. Some invest in long-term issues that increase the price of your individual shares but do not show as income on your statement.

Therefore, you might receive statements only when new activity that can be reflected on your account statement occurs in your fund. Check with your fund company to determine how often you should receive account statements.

You can calculate exactly how much your fund account is worth on a daily basis by checking your newspaper and multiplying the net asset value—the sell price per share—by the total number of shares you currently own.

> **Q:** **There are some mighty big funds out there. Should size be a consideration in my choice of funds?**

You can't operate a chicken farm with only ten chickens. The actual cost of keeping each hen would be prohibitive. Likewise, you can't optimize the major benefits of mutual-fund investing with limited funds to invest.

Economies of scale are important to reduce brokerage fees. Generous investor pools spread out risk by purchasing a larger number of securities. Extra cash on hand can be ready for investor redemptions and unexpected bargains without selling another security to raise cash.

On the other hand, some funds are so huge that they have great difficulty "beating the market." Let's face it: You can't beat the market if you *are* the market. What's more, stuffed with novice and unsophisticated investors out to "grab the money and exchange," these funds might be whip-sawed by greed and fear. Popular funds under pressure to produce consistently outstanding returns might carry little cash on hand.

> **Q:** **Are there advantages to investing in a mutual fund family?**

Investing "in the family way" allows you to move your money from one fund to another easily. This also allows you to invest in several funds at a time, receive consolidated statements, or switch from one fund to another with one phone call.

Consumers should invest primarily for performance, not convenience. Mutual fund companies, all of which have some mediocre or inferior products, love lazy consumers.

Do you visit one doctor for all your body parts? Do you eat only at one restaurant? Do you shop only at one store for all your purchases?

Of course not. Don't settle for convenience when long-term investment quality is more critical.

> **Q:** **If I do invest in a family and can exchange between funds, when should I switch?**

Hopefully, never. Find the optimum fund for your objectives and stay with it. Most small investors switch because they are losing money in their fund. They sell at a loss and move to another that looks more attractive, buying near that fund's peak.

If you are unhappy with your fund's performance, reevaluate your criteria for investing, choose another that affords less risk to principal and *stay put!*

> **Q:** **I can reinvest distributions into a different fund in the same family. Is this a good idea?**

Once you have found the optimum funds for your financial objectives, don't change directions unless you suddenly need current income or your financial life changes significantly.

This option is a marketing perk and should not be confused with good investing fundamentals.

> **Q:** **Every paper or magazine I read recommends a different list of funds. Which publications are right?**

If the so-called experts can't agree with one another—and none of them are correct on a consistent basis—it might be that there are no better experts than you.

Besides, magazines make lots of money from advertisements, and most financial publications are filled with ads from mutual funds. How inclined do you think they are to bite the hand that feeds them?

> **Q: Last year my fund returned 15%.
> This year—less than 2%. Should I
> sell it and find a better fund?**

Remember: you must take a longer-term view before drawing conclusions. Select those mutual funds that perform admirably during poor economic times, yet participate generously during the better periods.

> **Q: When does a load (sales charge)
> become a burden?**

Some mutual funds, called contractual plans, exact as much as 50 percent of the first year's investment in up-front charges. There is absolutely no justification for charges even as high as 8.5% of your investment principal. You can purchase high quality mutual funds for much less. You might need to pay something for top management. But when charges get that high, the load becomes too heavy to carry.

> **Q: Why should I pay anything? Why
> not just buy no-load funds?**

No one will invest your money for nothing. If they did, they could not pay their distribution costs, advertising, business overhead, or other expenses of doing business. But it sounds good to hear those promises.

A list of the cheapest funds available today would be different from my list of best performers. Buying on price alone is a costly mistake.

Do you visit only the cheapest doctors? Eat only at the cheapest restaurants? Are you driving the cheapest car on the road today or the one that is the best value?

Although a large price tag certainly does not ensure quality, a cheap one might cost you more in the end. Shop for your investments in the same manner you do for other consumer items. Find the best values for your dollars.

> **Q: My fund is hemorrhaging. Should I sell now, pay the steep surrender charge and eat my losses, or wait?**

There are greater losses to be feared if your fund takes a solid hit to its principal because it carried too much risk. Surrender charges are the real cost of the "free lunch" deferred sales charge you were told would "disappear" in a few years (the "back-end load"). Now they have come back to haunt you.

You paid those charges when you bought in, whether you saw them or not. How did the salesperson get paid? How did the company make its money? How can any company stay in business if everyone's charges "disappear" over time?

If there were no penalty for liquidation, would you leave today? If so, face reality and don't risk a lot for a little. Move to a lower-risk, well-diversified fund, regardless of any so-called back-door or up-front costs.

Chapter 5

Decoding
The
Mutual Fund
Prospectus

Now that your study of the newspaper's mutual fund page has interested you in one or more funds, it's time to do some more in-depth research. Call the companies whose funds you like and ask for prospectuses.

You'll probably think that they are written in a foreign language. Well, they aren't, but they might as well be since you're viewing something pored over, written, rewritten, and rewritten again by a team of legal beagles.

This chapter will help you understand this new foreign language.

A typical prospectus might sound like this:

> XYZ Company Agreement provides that the compensation of the Advisor will be reduced by the sum of its parts and divided by the number 13 (because that's my lucky number) plus the depreciation of the office furniture, assuming the reinvestment of all dividends and capital gains, and unless changed by a majority vote of the shareholders, upon the receipt of all proxies (and if you don't send them in the first time we will spend more of your money to send them to you again). In accordance with the investment objectives and policies of the Advisor to provide current income and growth of the brand-new shrubbery at the entrance to the lobby, that there

can be no assurance that XYZ will achieve its
original investment objectives (which are de-
fined in subsection 4-f-A2). However ....

A slight exaggeration, but not much! Is it any wonder that
consumers rely on newspapers and magazines to *tell* them
what funds to invest in? Who wouldn't feel daunted by such
gobbledygook?

I once heard a so-called financial advisor tell an audience
if they wanted a cheap solution to insomnia, keep some prospectuses by their bedside. His recommendation: don't bother
struggling through them. Poor advice, though you will need
some help to get started.

Q: Where do I start?

Most mutual funds have toll-free (800) telephone numbers.
Call information or visit your library for a complete listing.
The Investment Company Institute in Washington, D.C., is
the mutual fund industry's trade association. They can con-
nect you with individual funds and send their own helpful
general publications.

When your prospectuses arrive, be sure they are current.
Then check the minimum dollar requirement to open an
account. There is no sense reading about a fund that requires
$25,000 when you intent to start a $25-a-month college tuition
plan.

Also make sure you have received the correct prospectus.
There are some fund companies that offer several funds with
similar names. U.S. Government is a common term, and sector (single industry) funds may have several spin-offs from a
basic theme.

The Securities and Exchange Commission (SEC) has its
own disclaimer on the front cover, which states that it will not
approve or recommend any securities or guarantee the truth

of any prospectus statements even though they authorized the original fund to sell to the public.

This is a hint of just how far away they may be if your investment tanks and you are left with a leaky boat. It's up to you to "approve" or "disapprove" of a particular fund.

Q: What is the purpose of a prospectus?

The prospectus is your contract with the investment company that manages the mutual fund. It discloses the fund's investment policies and objectives, how it attempts to achieve its goals, most of the fees and expenses you might incur, and the risks, limitations, and special concerns inherent in the type of securities the fund purchases.

Also included is information on how to buy and sell shares, who the portfolio manager or investment advisors are, and the investment methods (or restrictions) employed.

Don't shy away from the technical and legal jargon. Until you are familiar with the underpinnings of a mutual fund, you are *not* ready to invest in it.

Stay awake—if you snooze, you could lose.

Q: When do we get to the good stuff—how the fund intends to make me rich?

The investment policy is key. If you are uncomfortable with terms such as "junk," "speculative," or "lower quality," (and you should be), discard any fund prospectus that liberally sprinkles such terms around.

If the investment policy states it seeks better-than-average stock returns, it will employ investment methods to strive for that goal, even if they increase risk to principal. A Statement that emphasizes current income over all else might place greater emphasis on yield than on safety of principal.

Since no fund can be all things, you must learn what secondary goals will be sacrificed to meet a primary objective. A fund seeking aggressive growth will struggle as the market declines, while one that emphasizes conservation of principal might return less than others in a raging bull market.

> ## Q: Where are the risks, limitations and dangers discussed?

Pore over any sections that contain that word "risk." You will find material data that a fund does not want to advertise in bold print, yet must disclose in its prospectus.

> ## Q: Where is the sticker price?

Prospectuses always include readily understandable fee tables. They discuss whether an investor will pay up-front charges (a front-end load), whether that load is invisible (a back-end load) and will supposedly disappear over several years or be charged when you liquidate, no matter *when* liquidation takes place.

Some funds have no up-front, back-load or redemption fees. These are called no-load funds, and many investors like this approach because they believe—wrongly—that someone will invest their money for nothing. No load does not mean no charges.

Some funds also charge a small (or not so small) annual distribution, or 12b-1, fee. The fund also must pay its advisors and cover administrative expenses.

> ## Q: How accurate are the tables and graphs in the sales literature?

They are supposed to be true historical performances. But good artwork and color can gussy up poor performance.

You shouldn't use a historical table to evaluate performance. Last year's winners could be this year's dogs. Expenses change, markets adjust (and correct), and no two years have the same dynamics.

> ## Q: Do I meet the money guru—my investment advisor?

You will find the name of your investment advisor, what he or she has been hired to do, and how much he or she charges. A profile is also available of the fund's transfer agent, appointed by the fund to maintain accurate records, prepare account statements, record tax information, and administer other shareholder services.

> ## Q: What rights do I have as a shareholder?

These are spelled out in the section that discusses ownership, voting privileges, and special methods of investing. All mutual funds are organized under similar statutes.

Volume discounts available, instructions for submitting a letter of intent, and when a signature guarantee is needed are detailed.

Q: What are rights of accumulation?

Some funds offer price discounts for volume purchases. For example, you might receive a lower price per share if your investment is more than $25,000. As your contributions grow and you accumulate earnings, when you reach a certain (breakpoint) figure, you will pay less per share from that time on, no matter how little you invest from then on.

Once you have reached a certain volume breakpoint, you will never be expected to pay full price, no matter how many different funds you choose in the same fund family or how your family accounts are titled.

Q: What is a letter of intent ?

Assume you want to invest $25,000 into one or more funds offered by the same investment company, but you don't have access to your money right now. Perhaps your CD will mature in three months, or your retirement pension will be distributed to you within the year. You could still receive a volume discount based on the total dollars you intend to invest in the next 13 months.

A *letter of intent* does not commit you to purchasing future shares. You declare that you will try, and you want the discount now. The mutual fund will trust you and reduce the current price of your shares, according to the amount you have declared you *might* invest. A letter of intent can also be backdated three months to reduce prices on an investment made in the recent past.

You have 13 months to fulfill your promise to invest the amount of money you promised. When you do, the fund will send you a "completion of letter of intent" statement. If you don't make your goal, the fund will sell a portion of your shares to make up for the discount, changing your original prices per share to the figures you would normally have paid. There is no additional cost for a letter of intent.

Make a reasonable decision when weighing the validity of a letter of intent. It is psychologically defeating to see your account value go down because the share prices have been adjusted after the deadline has passed.

Q: What is a signature guarantee?

When you liquidate a large account or redeem a qualified account such as an IRA, 403b or 401k, in writing, someone must vouch for your signature. A *signature guarantee* can be requested at a commercial bank, a federally chartered savings and loan, or a brokerage company. This authorization is stronger than a notary seal because the institution signing it is pledging their assets behind their stamp that declares you really are who you say you are.

This requirement is for the protection of each shareholder, although sometimes inconvenient. Call to ask whether your banking institution offers this service.

Q: How do I buy in?

How to purchase and redeem shares is fully discussed in any prospectus, including how to complete an application and to whom the check should be payable. If you are contributing to an IRA account or doing a pension retirement IRA rollover or another type of qualified account, ask for the pertinent applications.

Call the fund's shareholder service department if you need further assistance. They are your best source of accurate information. But when dealing with telephone representatives, stick to the primary reason you called them. Don't let anyone suggest their "breakfast special." You could be listening to a salespitch, not a helpful recommendation.

Chapter 6

Taxation, Representation And Mutual Funds

I hate taxes—not just paying them but also reading and writing about them. So this section is brief. You should always consult a tax expert for specific details, as laws and regulations surely will change before this ink dries.

Q: How will my mutual fund dividends be taxed?

At the beginning of the following year you will receive a 1099 (or 1099-R, similar to those from bank CDs or savings accounts, for IRA and other pension withdrawals), stating how much you earned in interest, dividends and/or capital gains from the securities sold by the fund during the year.

You are not currently taxed on any change in the price of your shares until you actually sell them.

If you redeem shares during the year, the difference between the original purchase price (their cost basis) and their current worth at the time of the sale will be taxed—if you made a profit.

If you sell them at a loss, you can deduct up to $3,000 per year until you have deducted the entire loss. Many funds provide data to simplify these calculations.

> ## Q: If I bought shares at different times, which ones are considered "sold" if I only sell a portion of them?

Ordinarily, the shares you bought first are the ones assumed sold. But if you specify which shares you want to sell before they are actually redeemed, you might reduce your taxes by selling shares that cost the same or more than the ones you sold.

Assume you bought 100 shares at $8 each several years ago. You bought 100 additional shares last year, and paid $12 each. Today all shares are worth $10 per share. You want to sell 100 shares now.

You could sell the shares without specifying which ones would be sold, in which case the FIFO ("First In, First Out) principle would apply. The IRS would assume you sold the $8 shares you purchased first. You would be taxed on $2 per share or $200 total profit in the year you sold them ($10 per share sale price minus $8 per share cost).

Or you could state in writing before the sale that you wished to sell the last 100 shares you purchased at $12 per share, resulting in a loss of $2 per share ($10/share - $12/share = $2/share loss). Selling 50 shares at $8 and 50 shares at $12 would be a wash—$0 profit, $0 loss.

Sooner or later, you will have to sell the cheaper shares. So consider your future tax liability before using such tax planning. Send a backup letter to your fund indicating exactly which shares are to be sold and maintain a copy in case the IRS later questions this sale.

> ## Q: Am I taxed if I exchange from one fund to another?

An exchange is treated as a sale and a new purchase. Whether you exchange your fund for another in the same family, move into a new fund family, or take the distribution in cash, you have a tax consequence unless you are protected by a tax shelter like an IRA.

> **Q: If I reinvest to buy new shares, am I taxed on my earnings?**

Whether you take your distributions and spend them, reinvest them, or invest in another fund, the tax liability is the same. The moment they are distributed to you they become taxable income.

> **Q: If my IRA account is in a mutual fund, how will it be taxed?**

All earnings in an IRA account are tax-deferred until withdrawal. If your original contributions were tax-deductible, they will also be taxed when you withdraw them. If you also have non-deductible contributions, they will not be taxed again. Earnings in either type of IRA are taxed only when you withdraw them.

If Uncle Sam didn't tax you on the funds you contributed to the IRA, he will tax you when you withdraw them.

> **Q: Can I choose which IRA money to withdraw?**

You must withdraw deductible and non-deductible IRA funds in proportion to your account value. If you are confused by these rules, get some assistance from a tax advisor, at least the first time you withdraw.

> **Q: What are the tax consequences of moving my IRA account into a mutual fund?**

If you maintain the IRA title on all funds, there are no current taxes. Just be sure to follow all IRA rollover rules.

> **Q: How does the IRS know where I have my IRA accounts anyway?**

When you transfer an IRA account, the custodian tells the IRS you took out your money. When you transfer through a special IRA application, the new custodian reports that the contribution came in. When both reports are compared, the IRS can see if all IRA funds are accounted for.

Mutual funds charge a nominal fee for IRA reporting. When you receive your first statement, check to be sure the IRA title has been noted. Any errors should be immediately reported to the fund and corrected as soon as possible. You have only 60 days to safely transfer your IRA account to the new custodian. ***Do not miss that deadline.***

> **Q: What if I withdraw my IRA funds before retirement age?**

If you withdraw IRA money before age 59 1/2, you will pay a 10% penalty in addition to the regular taxes on the amount you withdraw. Though that's is a stiff penalty, the power of tax deferral is so great that you should still contribute annually if you can, no matter how young you are.

> **Q: I am in the highest tax bracket and need some tax-fighting investments. How about tax-free bonds?**

Although you can sidestep the taxman if you choose (to a certain extent), consideration should be given to the riskier nature of tax-free bonds. Municipal bonds will suffer greater pressures in the next few years as federal and state funding for social programs and public projects shrinks.

In the highest tax bracket, you will give 33 cents of every dollar of investment profit to the government. Risky investments that default can cost you 100 cents of every dollar invested! Therefore, it might be more prudent to share your loaf of bread with the taxman than to go completely hungry if your tax-exempt investments default.

Chapter 7

How To
Buy The
Wrong
Mutual Fund

Small investors are usually in the wrong investment at the wrong time. As great opportunities are developing in the valley, the little guy is losing his breath climbing over the wrong hill.

There was almost no way around this sorry fate when the best investment vehicles could be driven only by the affluent. But now that mutual funds have given "average Joes and Janes" (like us!) access to a once exclusive investment menu, little guys have a better chance of finding the land of milk and honey.

Nevertheless, many small investors guarantee themselves a difficult financial road because they operate under a number of misconceptions. Here are eighteen of the most common mistakes small investors make—the eighteen strategies small investors should *avoid like the plague.*

1. Grab last year's top performer

During your next library visit, request back issues of popular consumer money magazines. Compare year-end results for the past five years. You'll see how rarely top performers do successful encores.

2. Select the most popular mutual fund category

The biotech industry funds burst onto the stage in 1991 to take the financial community by storm. It was love at first

sight. By 1992, though, after luring thousands of small investors into their ranks, they crashed and burned.

Drawn by the stories of quick profits, many novice investors bought near the top and lost their financial shirts as
those funds plummeted downhill.

Smart investors avoid faddish media-hyped sector (industry) mutual funds and those that invest in only one type of
security.

3. Choose the mutual fund with the highest year-to-date (current) return

A variation on the above theme, attempting to predict
investment performance from looking at one static point in
time is as faulty as calling a horse race soon after the gates
have opened. Some entries move out fast, then fade, while
others tend to be closers.

4. Use long-term performance as a reliable predictor of future returns

Many mutual funds tout their long-term records, but few
things are worth less than old news.

The fund with a 10-year track record of greatness might
have just seen its superstar manager walk off the job, or its
composition and investment style might have changed drasti-
cally.

When a mutual fund states in its prospectus that past
performance is no guarantee of future returns, bank on it.

5. Become seduced by sector (industry) funds

If a mutual fund family is racing 50 or more individual
entries, each focused on a specific sector of the economy, it is
impossible not to produce a winner once in a while. However,
if you examine a sector mutual fund performance graph, you
might mistake it for an EKG of a patient having a major heart
attack.

Sector funds are dangerous because they reduce meaning-ful diversification, thereby heightening risk to principal.

6. Concentrate on funds that invest only in stocks or only in bonds

The stock market can be a scary place if you are invested in it at the wrong time. And the bond markets can be every bit as volatile when interest rates begin creeping up.

The only safe method of investing is to formulate a well-rounded strategy—a portfolio of both quality stocks and high-grade bonds, surrounded by a healthy amount of cash, even when interest rates are low.

7. Choose funds for income when you really need growth

Anyone planning to live more than three years has an inflation problem. Always invest some of your assets in inflation fighters like equity income mutual funds. The best simulate a financial stew—it's all in there. From bank CDs, cash, and Treasury bills, to familiar stocks, corporate bonds, and even long-term U.S. government bonds, these funds are as broad-based as a millionaire's portfolio.

8. Chase after higher yields in today's low interest rate environment

Scrambling for higher yields today isn't smarter banking. It's flirting with death.

You should avoid shopping with any eye on yields alone. Many investments offering relief from low-interest sticker shock contain international bonds or other, more risky debt obligations to produce those higher returns.

Are you comfortable with some of your dollars in the Tasmanian waterworks? Perhaps a Nova Scotian public facil-ity? You must thoroughly read the mutual fund's prospectus for risks, exclusions, special investment methods, or other warning signs that might not have been fully disclosed (or even understood) by the fund salesperson.

9. Purchase a fund because of its reputation

That's a fine way to buy burgers and chickens, but a lousy way to buy investments. Sure, you must go with a solid, well-performing fund. But make sure it's not one that everybody and his sister has already invested in.

10. "Diversify" your portfolio by picking funds from a single family

No one corners the market on financial expertise and quality investments. Every mutual fund company has mediocre selections, and most of them have some real dogs.

Therefore, you should choose your funds as you would your best friends, from the whole world of investment opportunities, even if it is cheaper or more convenient to stick with one company. Nobody does it all—at least not well.

11. Trade funds for short-term returns, always looking for the "quick profit"

With my risk-adverse attitude, I would be a terrible spy. If captured, one look at an 8 x 10 glossy of Edward Scissorhands, and I would spill everything, even my real age (or hair color).

But please overlook my squeamishness as I insist that switching among funds trying to make a killing is more likely to kill you!

12. Choose mutual funds that use market-timing strategies

Asset allocation or timing funds are an offshoot of the greedy '80s. Steeped in the euphoria of double-digit returns year after year, many investors forgot about the laws of gravity while they temporarily floated on a financial Cloud 9.

Nobody can attain stratospheric returns and outperform the averages for very long, especially without utilizing risky leveraging or other questionable management strategies. Anyone who could successfully predict market swings based on events which have not yet happened should make you wonder what kind of voodoo is going on behind those inviting brochures and scintillating promises.

Stick to the KISS theory (Keep it Simple, Stupid) and focus on creating *less* risk, not opting for more.

13. Choose funds that are known targets for market timers and "switching" newsletters

Nothing produces stomach acid more quickly for portfolio managers than seeing 50,000 redemption slips on Monday morning, right after all assets have been fully invested. Large influxes of new investment capital or unexpected mass redemptions make it virtually impossible to develop long-term investment strategies.

Many famous stock or bond funds tend to be 100% invested in stocks or bonds at all times. No matter when the public showers the company with expectant dollars, the manager must buy something, whether or not the timing is prudent.

Therefore, you should avoid funds that significantly shrink from investor flight or bloat with waves of new money based on open recommendations to the general public.

14. Buy a fund with less than a five-year track record

New mutual funds spring up almost daily, but you cannot tell how well a product will perform in different economic conditions until it has ridden out some stormy seas. There's *no* good reason to expose your principal to unnecessary risk.

15. Purchase on recommendations from consumer publications

You can't find today's thoroughbred track winners with yesterday's racing form. Similarly, you can't pick tomorrow's top-performing mutual funds by looking backward at data that might already be several months old by the time it shows up in print.

The factors that go into smart long-term investment decisions among a multitude of investment options are far too complex to be boiled down to A,B,C, or D ratings on a magazine page.

Such ratings often lead unwitting investors to invest in funds just as they are peaking.

If profits depended on alphabetical ratings, most of us would find it ever so easy to be filthy rich.

16. Buy on the advice of friends, colleagues, co-workers or relatives

I remember a cartoon depicting a formal dinner attended by successful bank executives. Each guest was sharing tidbits of information with the banker to his or her right. As the butler finished serving the first course, he whisked into the kitchen and announced to the staff: "Quick! Sell your industrials! More to come during the entree."

Most consumers have little idea what they are invested in, the real returns on their investment choices, or whether their products will work in their unique situation. Before you are quick to rely on the advice of others, ask yourself what these helpful folks do for a living.

Well-meaning incompetents can damage your financial future as surely as any vested interest could. Use your own brand of research, common sense instincts, the KISS theory, and lots of diversification.

17. Believe that "no load" means "no charges"

No one will invest your money for nothing. End of story. Any attempts to believe otherwise are naive. You are going to pay charges, whether you see them or not, even if you avoid front-end loads (up-front charges), back-end loads (deferred charges that supposedly wear off after so many years), or even 12 b-1 fees.

Funds want assets to manage, and they will compete for your dollars even if they have to use special marketing methods to do so.

All mutual funds, regardless of the methods they use, have internal fees, overhead expense, advertising budgets, employees to pay, and distribution expenses other than the management fees you see in the prospectus. So the term "no load" means only that you see no up-front charge (though their expenses might be detailed in other areas of the prospectus such as the Condensed Financial Information and Additional Statement).

If visible charges bother you, some funds will be happy to remove them from your eyes to make you more comfortable and imply they have completely disappeared.

Be wary of mutual fund companies that promise you a free ride.

18. Purchase any fund without reading and understanding the prospectus

Mutual funds must disclose technical but vital information. This is compiled into a prospectus, a flimsy brochure in small print that many investors ignore to save time and, sometimes, their sanity.

Don't let technical terms deter you from learning. The prospectus is a legal document—there are severe penalties for material misstatements or critical omissions. If you cannot understand the prospectus, you are not ready to invest.

While the bold print giveth, the fine print could taketh away. Always separate the salespitch from the facts by reading and thoroughly understanding your investment contract, the prospectus.

Chapter 8

So You Think You're Ready To Invest

Before you sink your money into stocks, bonds, CDs or even mutual funds, here are the answers to several more questions you might not have thought to ask.

Q: What makes markets move up and down?

Good news, bad news, and no news at all. Markets lurch forward or languish for lack of support due to the cost of borrowed money, the leverage of a company trying to expand, the promise of a new product or service (or one that *doesn't* appear), rumors that trickle down through investment circles, the consumer price index, unemployment claims, fear of inflation, the discount rate, the public confidence level, and, once in a while, just the belief that rock 'n' roll will never die.

No matter what anyone tells you, markets are *not* rational. They respond to the two most prevalent psychoses of investors: greed and fear.

Q: Does a fund's previous long-term success indicate it will be a good performer for me?

It all depends on when the mutual fund performed well. Funds invested in the stock market will struggle when stocks are out of favor. Bonds will falter when interest rates are ris - ing.

I invest with a different eye. I look for the risks instead of the rewards. If you search out funds that perform well during tough times, then you'll smooth out your financial highway.

Q: I'm an investment wimp. Is there a mutual fund for me?

Mutual funds are broken down into categories, depending on the investments they hold. If you can find those that invest in a little of everything—equity income funds—you will have the diversification of a millionaire's portfolio.

Sometimes it takes a leap of faith to get started. So do your homework, then invest a little at a time. These funds will be around for a long time. Slowly, information will replace the fear you currently feel, and you will eventually be investing as confidently as the pros.

Q: Can I purchase real estate through mutual funds?

Funds that invest in real property offer the small investor the profit potential associated with real estate moguls. But disastrous experiences with (severely) limited partnerships taught us that becoming a land baron is not synonymous with bringing home the big bucks.

I recommend you invest no more than one-third of your total assets in real estate of any kind, including your own home. Consumers are often already overloaded because they bought too much house, believing it was the best investment they could make. If you own a $100,000 home, do you have a balance of $200,000 in other types of investments at your fingertips?

Buying even more real estate with significant downside risk and possible long waits between market adjustments is not prudent diversification. Investors would be better served with less complicated and more direct ownership of real estate assets.

Q: Is a fund that returned 40% last year better than one which made only 20%?

Maybe not. Funds that do well in easy economic environments rarely perform well during the tough times. What does it take to make 40% in one year? Maybe a greater risk than you realize and are prepared to take.

Choose your mutual funds from those that perform best during downturns, rather than in an environment of easy profits. If you focus on these winners, you will also profit during good periods.

Q: My fund manager is a superstar. Is the best management what counts most?

The captain of the Titanic had little power to move the iceberg away from the ship's path. Every stock fund superstar manager lost fund assets in the Crash of 1987, the correction of 1989, and during stock market downturns.

If your fund is heavily invested in a volatile investment category, a whole slew of superstars couldn't save you. They may respond quickly, but they cannot totally avoid or control major market corrections.

Remember that investment performance depends primarily on the type of investment, not the manager. Find the well-diversified mutual funds first. Then choose one with a quality manager.

> **Q: If I choose from last year's top funds will I guarantee myself a winner?**

A buy-and-hold philosophy works much better. Purchase quality and well-diversified mutual fund "turtles," those equity income types, and let the jackrabbits whiz by. You may later see the hot funds lying at the side of the road, exhausted, while you continue your slow and steady race toward the accumulation of wealth.

> **Q: What are closed-end funds? How do they differ from other funds?**

First, let's define their opposite. Open-end funds (commonly called mutual funds) are not traded like stocks and bonds on an open market auction. They are purchased directly from the mutual fund investment company in the form of shares, then redeemed directly back to them when you want to liquidate part or all of your account value.

The price of shares fluctuates daily according to the total value of all securities inside the mutual funds. They are actively managed by a portfolio manager or management team who do the actual security selection. The funds store any shareholder profits until the next distribution period.

The value of each share is proportional to the total asset value divided by the number of shares in investors' possession, called the shares outstanding.

Closed-end funds, on the other hand, are packaged, then sold to investors. They are traded on an open market at prices that fluctuate with investor popularity and perception of value. They may sell at prices below or above the market value of the securities they hold. Investor demand moves the value of closed-end funds.

An additional distinction separates closed-end funds from the ordinary mutual funds most investors know. Once they are packaged, they are no longer actively managed. They roll with the punches during changing markets and through various economic periods, similar to stocks.

Would a large company hire a management team to organize the basic structure and corporate mission, then fire all its executives, expecting the company to run itself? How would you feel if your airline pilot stepped off the plane just before take-off?

For these reasons, I recommend that you stay with open-ended mutual funds as they are easier to evaluate and to price. I prefer rowing my own raft over the rapids to sitting down in the bottom of the boat, closing my eyes, and praying for a safe landing.

> **Q: When new investors purchase my mutual fund, does that increase the price of my shares?**

Mutual funds exchange investor money for new shares they issue. Then they invest that new money into securities. So the price of your shares depends on the value of all the securities held by your mutual funds, not on how many investors are buying in or redeeming their shares.

> ## Q: Why does my mutual fund go down when it distributes a dividend or a capital gain?

If your fund dips well below its normal price range, look in your newspaper for a small (x) or (e). That means the fund has distributed cash to its investors. If this is so, you can either receive that cash or reinvest to purchase additional shares of the fund.

Assume you have $100 in a bank account, and your lender sends you $20 of it. You now have $80 in your account and a $20 check in your hand. You may spend or reinvest that $20. If you choose to reinvest it, you have the same $100 you started with.

You make no profits when the fund actually distributes a dividend, interest or a capital gain. You are simply receiving part of your account value. Right after the distribution, the old account value is worth that much less, whether you have the distribution in your pocket or instruct your mutual fund to reinvest it into new shares (or shares of another mutual fund in the same fund family).

> ## Q: If I reinvest my distribution profits can I lose the money I already made?

Your price per share will continue to move up and down in value, including any additional shares purchased. When you reinvest, you convert cash back into new shares, purchased at the price available when you buy them. If the net asset value later declines below the original cost, your new shares could be worth less than you paid for them.

Don't be alarmed by this possibility; you are investing for the long-term. If you have chosen your funds in a prudent and conservative manner, price changes should be minimal and adjust upward during more favorable economic periods.

> **Q:** **I'm getting a high yield on my mutual fund, but my share price is going down. What's happening?**

Will Rogers said a mouthful when he stated that the return *of* his money was every bit as important as any return *on* his money. You should be concerned because some funds will keep an attractive yield going even if they have to shrink your principal to do so.

There are two parts to any investment: (1) the return or yield on your investment money, and (2) what is happening to your principal. When you consistently see your share price deteriorating, that means the fund is distributing higher yields than the actual securities inside are producing, and you are losing investment principal.

There is more to smart investing today than shopping for yields. Find a mutual fund that does not compete by managing your money so aggressively. Look for one that is more in line with current interest rates on the types of securities in which it invests. Funds that manage for total return (instead of luring you in with hot returns) do a better job of protecting your investment principal as markets adjust over time.

These will reduce the returns (yield) in line with economic changes instead of hoping you don't notice your shrinking capital and placating you with unrealistic high returns.

Index